Invasive Exotic Plant Monitoring at Pea Ridge National Military Park: Year 1 (2006)

Natural Resource Report NPS/HTLN/NRTR—2007/019
NPS D-49

Craig C. Young, J. Tyler Cribbs, Jennifer L. Haack, and Holly J. Etheridge
National Park Service, Heartland I&M Network
Wilson's Creek National Battlefield, 6424 West Farm Road 182, Republic, MO 65738

Heartland Network
Natural Resource Monitoring

March 2007

U.S. Department of the Interior
National Park Service
Natural Resource Program Center
Fort Collins, Colorado

The Natural Resource Publication series addresses natural resource topics that are of interest and applicability to a broad readership in the National Park Service and to others in the management of natural resources, including the scientific community, the public, and the NPS conservation and environmental constituencies. Manuscripts are peer-reviewed to ensure that the information is scientifically credible, technically accurate, appropriately written for the intended audience, and is designed and published in a professional manner.

The Natural Resource Technical Report series is used to disseminate the peer-reviewed results of scientific studies in the physical, biological, and social sciences for both the advancement of science and the achievement of the National Park Service's mission. The reports provide contributors with a forum for displaying comprehensive data that are often deleted from journals because of page limitations. Current examples of such reports include the results of research that addresses natural resource management issues; natural resource inventory and monitoring activities; resource assessment reports; scientific literature reviews; and peer reviewed proceedings of technical workshops, conferences, or symposia.

Views and conclusions in this report are those of the authors and do not necessarily reflect policies of the National Park Service. Mention of trade names or commercial products does not constitute endorsement or recommendation for use by the National Park Service.

Printed copies of reports in these series may be produced in a limited quantity and they are only available as long as the supply lasts. This report is also available from the Heartland I&M Network website (http://www.nature.nps.gov/im/units/HTLN) on the internet, or by sending a request to the address on the back cover.

Please cite this publication as:

Young, C.C, J.T. Cribbs, J.L. Haack, and H.J. Etheridge. 2007. Invasive exotic plant monitoring at Pea Ridge National Military Park: Year 1 (2006). Natural Resource Technical Report NPS/HTLN/NRTR—2007/019. National Park Service, Fort Collins, Colorado.

NPS D-49, March 2007

Acknowledgements

Dan Tenaglia conducted all field work associated with this report in 2006. Dan died on February 13, 2007 following a collision two days earlier while riding his bike near his home in Opelika, Alabama. We are grateful for his work. Dan's botanical photography can be found at his Missouri Plants website: http://www.missouriplants.com/.

Executive Summary

During surveys in 2006, we documented 13 invasive, exotic plant species and the native Eastern red cedar on Pea Ridge National Military Park. The survey focused on the relatively mature forests at the park to the exclusion of old fields and successional forests. Within these forests, six invasive exotic plant species were not previously documented in NPSpecies, as occurring on the park. Eastern redcedar, covering between 671 and 1152 acres, was by far the most abundant plant documented in the survey. Out of the 13 species identified, six species occupied less than one acre. In general, only a few invasive exotic plants pose a problem in the park's forest. We suspect that smooth brome, Nepalese browntop, and knapweed are invasive plant species that may not have previously come to the attention of park managers. The acreage estimates presented in the report may be used to plan management activities leading to control of exotic plants and accomplishment of GPRA goal IA1b.

Table of Contents

Introduction

Author's note. In this report, we use the term invasive exotic plant to refer to plants that are not native to the park and that are presumed to pose environmental harm to native plant populations and/or communities based on a review of numerous state and regional invasive exotic plant lists. The great majority of the introductory text was taken from Welch and Geissler (2007) with slight modification.

Scope of invasive exotic plant problem for National Parks. Globalization of commerce, transportation, human migration, and recreation in recent history has introduced invasive exotic species to new areas at an unprecedented rate. Biogeographical barriers that once restricted the location and expansion of species have been circumvented, culminating in the homogenization of the Earth's biota. Although only 10% of introduced species become established and only 1% become problematic (Williamson 1993, Williamson and Fitter 1996) or invasive, nonnative species have profound impacts worldwide on the environment, economies, and human health. Invasive species have been directly linked to the replacement of dominant native species (Tilman 1999), the loss of rare species (King 1985), changes in ecosystem structure, alteration of nutrient cycles and soil chemistry (Ehrenfeld 2003), shifts in community productivity (Vitousek 1990), reduced agricultural productivity, and changes in water availability (D'Antonio and Mahall 1991). Often the damage caused by these species to natural resources is irreparable and our understanding of the consequences incomplete. Invasive species are second only to habitat destruction as a threat to wildland biodiversity (Wilcove et al. 1998). Consequently, the dynamic relationships among plants, animals, soil, and water established over many thousands of years are at risk of being destroyed in a relatively brief period.

For the National Park Service (NPS), the consequences of these invasions present a significant challenge to the management of the agency's natural resources "unimpaired for the enjoyment of future generations." National Parks, like other land management organizations, are deluged by new exotic species arriving through predictable (e.g., road, trail, and riparian corridors), sudden (e.g., long-distance dispersal through cargo containers and air freight), and unexpected anthropogenic pathways (e.g., weed seeds in restoration planting mixes). Nonnative plants claim an estimated 4,600 acres of public lands each year in the United States (Asher and Harmon 1995), significantly altering local flora. For example, exotic plants comprise an estimated 43% and 36% of the flora of the states of Hawaii and New York, respectively (Rejmanek and Randall 1994). Invasive plants infest an estimated 2.6 million acres of the 83 million acres managed by the NPS.

More NPS lands are infested daily despite diligent efforts to curtail the problem. Impacts from invasive species have been realized in most parks, resulting in an expressed need to control existing infestations and restore affected ecosystems. Additionally, there is a growing urgency to be proactive—to protect resources not yet impacted by current and future invasive species (Marler 1998). Invasive exotic species most certainly will continue to be a management priority for the National Parks well into the 21st Century. Invasive exotic plants have been consistently ranked as a top vital sign for long term monitoring as part of the NPS Inventory & Monitoring (I&M) Program. During the vital signs selection process in 2003, Heartland Network parks recognized the need for exotic plant monitoring (DeBacker et al. 2004). Nine parks (CUVA,

EFMO, GWCA, HEHO, HOCU, HOME, LIBO, OZAR, PERI) identified invasive exotic plants as their most important management issue, two parks (TAPR, WICR) identified invasive exotic plants as their second most important management issue, and PIPE identified invasive exotic plants as its third most important management issue. During this process, invasive exotic plant monitoring was recognized across all network parks as the most important shared monitoring need.

Prevention and early detection as keys to invasive exotic plant management. Prevention and early detection are the principal strategies for successful invasive exotic plant management. While there is a need for long-term suppression programs to address very high-impact species, eradication efforts are most successful for infestations less than one hectare in size (Rejmanek and Pitcairn 2002). Eradication of infestations larger than 100 hectares is largely unsuccessful, costly, and unsustainable (Rejmanek and Pitcairn 2002). Costs, or impacts, to ecosystem components and processes resulting from invasion also increase dramatically over time, making ecosystem restoration improbable in the later stages of invasion. Further, in their detailed review of the nonnative species problem in the United States, the US Congress, Office of Technology Assessment (1993) stated that the environmental and economic benefits of supporting prevention and early detection initiatives significantly outweigh any incurred costs, with the median benefit-to-cost ratio being 17:1 in favor of being proactive.

Although preventing the introduction of invasive exotic plants is the most successful and preferred strategy for resource managers, the realities of globalization, tight fiscal constraints, and limited staff time guarantee that invaders will get through park borders. Fortunately, invasive exotic plants quite often undergo a lag period between introduction and subsequent colonization of new areas. Managers, then, can take advantage of early detection monitoring to make certain invasive exotic species are found and successfully eradicated before populations become well established.

This strategy requires resource managers to: (1) detect invasive exotic species early (i.e., find a new species or an incipient population of an existing species while the infestation is small (less than 1 hectare), and (2) respond rapidly (i.e., implement appropriate management techniques to eliminate the invasive plant and all of its associated regenerative material).

Invasive exotic plant management at Pea Ridge National Military Park. While a complete history of park invasive exotic plant management issues is beyond the scope of this report, a few important highlights are given:

1. Eastern redcedar (*Juniperus virginiana*) is very abundant in the forests at Pea Ridge National Military Park.

2. Sericea lespedeza (*Lespedeza cuneata*) is known to occur in disturbed areas, such as access roads, at the park.

3. The fields at Pea Ridge National Military Park support numerous exotic weeds, including a portion that may be characterized as invasive.

Methods

Watch lists. The invasive exotic plants on three watch lists were sought during monitoring (Table 1). Invasive exotic plants not known to occur on the park based on NPSpecies, the national NPS database for plant occurrence registration, constitute the early detection watch list. Invasive exotic plants known to occur on the park based on NPSpecies constitute the park-established watch list. Invasive exotic plants from the park-based watch list included plants selected by park managers or network staff which may not have been included on the other lists due to incomplete information in NPSpecies (e.g., not documented) or USDA Plants (e.g., state distribution information inaccurate) databases or due to differing opinions regarding network designation of a plant as a high priority. While aquatic species are listed on the watch lists, terrestrial plants were the focus of this survey. Aquatic plants were documented occasionally.

Field methods. Invasive exotic plant species on designated watch lists (Table 1) were sought in high priority areas on Pea Ridge National Military Park (Figure 1). The grassland and early successional forests on the park were excluded from this survey. The outlying land parcel was also not surveyed. Dan Tenaglia, the contract botanist for this project, used a Thales GPS unit to navigate along 400 m line transects, identified invasive exotic plants in an approximately 6-m belt, and attributed a coarse cover value to each species (0=0, 1=0.1-0.9 m^2, 2=1-9.9 m^2, 3=10-49.9 m^2, 4= 50-99.9 m^2, 5=100-499.9 m^2, 6= 499.9-999.9 m^2, 7=1,000-4,999.9 m^2, 8=5,000-9,999.9 m^2, and 9=10,000-14,999.9 m^2). A total of 101 transects were surveyed at Pea Ridge National Military Park. In some cases, line transects were clipped at park boundaries or by areas not surveyed. The number of transects as categorized by length were as follows: 0 m-100 m = 6; 100 m-200 m = 18; 200 m-300 m = 11; and 300 m-400 m = 66. The observer had discretion to search a larger belt if feasible, to search additional areas up to a 400 m perpendicular distance from the transect, to target locations likely to support exotic plants (e.g., field edges, roads), and to circumvent extremely difficult or hazardous terrain when needed. However, in most cases, the observer maintained the established line transect. Cover was estimated for all plants observed while navigating along the transect (i.e., not restricted to the 6-m belt).

Analytical methods. Data analysis involved simple displays, as well as calculation of plant frequency and cover. The invasive exotic plants encountered on Pea Ridge National Military Park were attributed to line transects in a GIS. Polygons surrounding occupied line transects were highlighted on maps for each invasive exotic plant encountered (Figures 2 – 15). Note that entire polygons were not fully searched. The park-wide frequency of invasive exotic plants was calculated as the percentage of occupied transects. A park-wide cover range was estimated using the high and low values of the cover classes for each invasive exotic plant encountered, assuming that 3 % of the park was searched and that the areas searched were representative of the entire park.

Invasiveness ranks. In order to provide additional information on the ecological impact and feasibility of control, the ecological impact and general management difficulty sub-ranks that constitute the invasiveness rank (I-rank), as determined by NatureServe (Morse et al. 2004), were listed when available. The ecological impact characterizes the effect of the plant on ecosystem processes, community composition and structure, native plant and animal populations, and the conservation significance of threatened biodiversity. General management difficulty ranks are assigned based on the resources and time generally required to control a plant, the non-target effects of control on native populations, and the accessibility of invaded sites. Sub-ranks are given as high (H), medium (M), low (L), insignificant (I), unknown (U), or a combination of ranks.

Results and Discussion

In 2006, a total of 13 invasive exotic plant taxa were found during the survey at Pea Ridge National Military Park (Table 2). Based on a park request, the native Eastern red cedar (*Juniperus virginiana*) was also identified on the park. Of these plants, eight taxa were known to occur on the park based on the NPSpecies database. The six plant species on the early detection watch list were not recognized in NPSpecies as occurring on the park, although park managers may already be aware of their presence. The species identified on the early detection list will be entered in NPSpecies and should subsequently be included on the park-established watch list.

The distribution and abundance of the invasive exotic plant species at Pea Ridge National Military Park varied widely. The native Eastern redcedar was widespread and abundant. The tree was estimated to cover between 671 and 1152 acres and occurred on 42.8% of transects. In general, the cover and distribution of invasive exotic plants was relatively low in the forested portions of Pea Ridge National Military Park. Sericea lespedeza (*Lespedeza cuneata*) covered between six and 20 acres. Japanese honeysuckle (*Lonicera japonica*) and multiflora rose (*Rosa multiflora*), comprising at least 2.9 and 2.2 acres respectively, were found to occur in 18.5% and 19.1% of the surveyed transects. The remaining 10 invasive exotic plant species each covered less than three acres and were encountered relatively infrequently.

Based on field observations, we believe that the cover of Eastern redcedar may have been systematically overestimated. Such overestimation likely resulted from difficulty estimating high cover over the 400 m transects. While such overestimation may complicate detection of change in the future, the relative size of cover estimates provides a strong basis for management planning.

No species were noted as having definitively high ecological impact. Black locust (*Robinia pseudoacacia*) was characterized as having a high to medium ecological impact (Table 2), but was only established on less than one acre. Eight species were characterized as having medium or medium-low ecological impacts. Japanese honeysuckle (*Lonicera japonica*), Nepalese browntop (*Microstegium vimineum*), Johnsongrass (*Sorghum halepense*), spotted knapweed (*Centaurea stoebe ssp. micranthos*), and Canada bluegrass (*Poa compressa*) were noted as being potentially difficult to manage, while management difficulty was medium or less for the remaining species. Management of the small invasive exotic populations on Pea Ridge National Military Park may well limit the costs and ecological impacts associated with the spread of these species.

In summary, this report provides information on invasive, exotic plant abundance and distribution. The report also characterizes the ecological impacts and management difficulty of these plants to assist park natural resource managers in planning invasive exotic plant management. The following links may further assist managers:
http://www.nature.nps.gov/im/units/htln/monitoring/projects/inp.htm and
http://www.natureserve.org/explorer/.

Literature Cited

Asher, J. A., and D. W. Harmon. 1995. Invasive exotic plants are destroying the naturalness of U.S. Wilderness areas. International Journal of Wilderness 1:35-37.

D'Antonio, C. M., and B. E. Mahall. 1991. Root profiles and competition between the invasive, exotic perennial, *Carpobrotus edulis,* and two native shrub species in California coastal scrub. American Journal of Botany 78:885-894.

DeBacker, M.D., C.C. Young (editor), P. Adams, L. Morrison, D. Peitz, G.A. Rowell, M. Williams, and D. Bowles. 2005. Heartland Inventory and Monitoring Network and Prairie Cluster Prototype Monitoring Program Vital Signs Monitoring Plan. National Park Service, Heartland Inventory and Monitoring Network and Prairie Cluster Prototype Monitoring Program, Wilson's Creek National Battlefield, Republic, Missouri, 104 pp. plus appendices.

Ehrenfeld, J.G. 2003. The effects of exotic plant invasions on soil nutrient cycling processes. Ecosystems 6:503-523.

King, W. B. 1985. Island birds: will the future repeat the past? Pages 3-15 *in* P. J. Moors, editor. Conservation of Island Birds. International Council for Bird Preservation. Cambridge University Press, Cambridge, UK.

Marler, M. 1998. Exotic plant invasions of federal Wilderness areas: current status and future directions. The Aldo Leopold Wilderness Research Institute. Rocky Mountain Research Station, Missoula, Montana, USA.

Office of Technology Assessment. 1993. Harmful non-indigenous species in the United States. OTA-F-565. U.S. Congress, Government Printing Office, Washington, D.C., USA.

Rejmanek, M., and M. J. Pitcairn. 2002. When is eradication of exotic pest plants a realistic goal? Pages 249-253 in C. R. Veitch and M. N. Clout, editors. Turning the Tide: the Eradication of Invasive Species. IUCN SSC Invasive Species Specialist Group. IUCN, Gland, Switzerland and Cambridge, UK.

Rejmanek, M., and J. M. Randall. 1994. Invasive alien plants in California: 1993 summary and comparison with other areas in North America. Madrono 41:161–177.

Tilman, D. 1999. The ecological consequences of changes in biodiversity: a search for general principles. Ecology 80:1455-1474.

Vitousek, P. M. 1990. Biological invasions and ecosystem processes: towards an integration of population biology and ecosystem studies. Oikos 57:7-13.

Welch, B.A. and P.H. Geissler. 2007. Early detection of invasive plants: a handbook. United States Geological Survey draft. http://www.pwrc.usgs.gov/brd/invasiveHandbook.cfm.

Wilcove, D. S., D. Rothstein, J. Dubow, A. Phillips, and E. Losos. 1998. Quantifying threats to imperiled species in the United States. Bioscience 48:607–615.

Williamson, M. 1993. Invaders, weeds and risk from genetically modified organisms. Experientia 49:219–224.

Williamson, M. and A. Fitter. 1996. The varying success of invaders. Ecology 77:1661–1666.

Pea Ridge National Military Park
Exotic Plant Search Line Transects

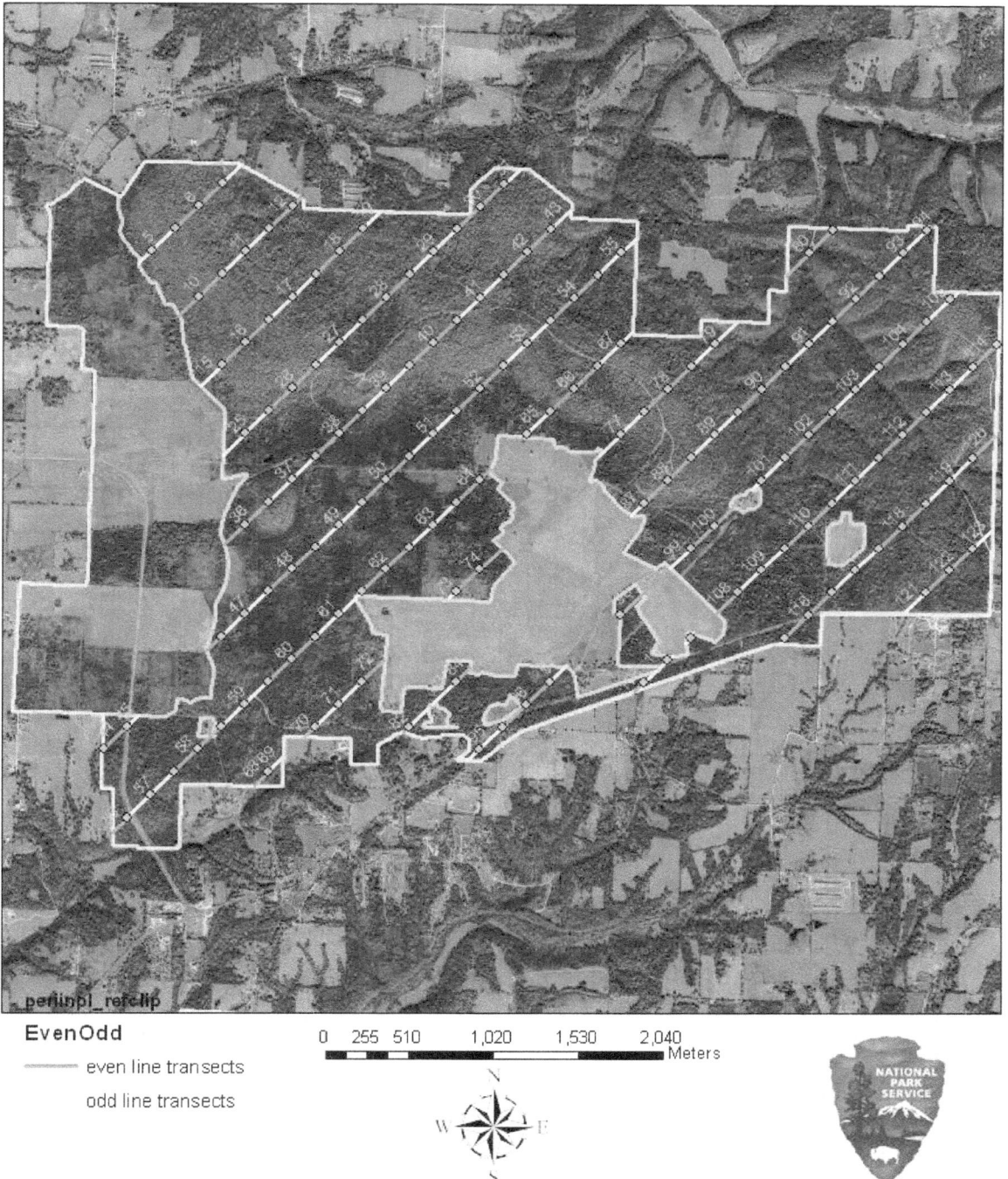

EvenOdd

⎯⎯ even line transects

odd line transects

perinpl_refclip

0   255 510   1,020   1,530   2,040
                                          Meters

N
W   E
S

Figure 1. Invasive exotic plant line transects at Pea Ridge National Military Park. The blue (even numbered) and orange (odd numbered) transects indicate the search locations for invasive exotic plants in 2006.

Table 1. Watch lists for Pea Ridge National Military Park

Early Detection Watch List		Park-Established Watch List		Park-Based Watch List	
Alliaria petiolata	Garlic mustard	Ailanthus altissima	Tree of heaven	Juniperus virginiana*	Eastern redcedar
Alternanthera philoxeroides	Alligatorweed	Albizia julibrissin	Silktree		
Alternanthera sessilis	Sessile joyweed	Bromus tectorum	Cheatgrass		
Ampelopsis brevipedunculata	Amur peppervine	Celastrus orbiculatus	Oriental bittersweet		
Arctium minus	Lesser burdock	Cirsium vulgare	Bull thistle		
Arundo donax	Giant reed	Cynodon dactylon	Bermudagrass		
Azolla	Mosquitofern	Dactylis glomerata	Orchardgrass		
Baccharis halimifolia	Eastern baccharis	Dioscorea oppositifolia	Chinese yam		
Bothriochloa bladhii	Caucasian bluestem	Echinochloa crus-galli	Barnyardgrass		
Bromus inermis	Smooth brome	Euonymus fortunei	Winter creeper		
Bromus sterilis	Poverty brome	Glechoma hederacea	Ground ivy		
Carduus nutans	Nodding plumeless thistle	Hedera helix	English ivy		
Centaurea stoebe ssp. micranthos	Spotted knapweed	Lespedeza cuneata	Sericea lespedeza		
Cirsium arvense	Canada thistle	Lonicera japonica	Japanese honeysuckle		
Dipsacus fullonum	Fuller's teasel	Lotus corniculatus	Bird's-foot trefoil		
Egeria densa	Brazilian waterweed	Melilotus officinalis	Yellow sweetclover		
Eichhornia crassipes	Common water hyacinth	Morus alba	White mulberry		
Elaeagnus pungens	Thorny olive	Paulownia tomentosa	Princesstree		
Elaeagnus umbellata	Autumn olive	Plantago lanceolata	Narrowleaf plantain		
Eragrostis curvula	Weeping lovegrass	Poa pratensis	Kentucky bluegrass		
Hesperis matronalis	Dames rocket	Populus alba	White poplar		
Holcus lanatus	Common velvetgrass	Potentilla recta	Sulphur cinquefoil		
Humulus japonicus	Japanese hop	Rhamnus cathartica	Common buckthorn		
Hydrilla verticillata	Waterthyme	Robinia pseudoacacia	Black locust		
Imperata cylindrica	Cogongrass	Rosa multiflora	Multiflora rose		
Lespedeza bicolor	Shrub lespedeza	Sorghum halepense	Johnsongrass		
Ligustrum lucidum	Glossy privet	Verbascum thapsus	Common mullein		
Ligustrum sinense	Chinese privet	Vinca major	Bigleaf periwinkle		
Ligustrum vulgare	European privet	Vinca minor	Common periwinkle		
Schedonorus phoenix	Tall fescue				
Schedonorus pratensis	Meadow fescue				
Lonicera maackii	Amur honeysuckle				
Lonicera morrowii	Morrow's honeysuckle				
Lygodium japonicum	Japanese climbing fern				
Lysimachia nummularia	Creeping jenny				
Lythrum salicaria	Purple loosestrife				
Melia azedarach	Chinaberrytree				
Microstegium vimineum	Nepalese browntop				
Murdannia keisak	Wartremoving herb				

Table 1. Watch lists for Pea Ridge National Military Park (cont.)

Early Detection Watch List		Park-Established Watch List	Park-Based Watch List
Myriophyllum aquaticum	Parrot feather watermilfoil		
Myriophyllum spicatum	Eurasian watermilfoil		
Nandina domestica	Sacred bamboo		
Pastinaca sativa	Wild parsnip		
Phalaris arundinacea	Reed canarygrass		
Photinia serratifolia	Taiwanese photinia		
Phragmites australis	Common reed		
Poa compressa	Canada bluegrass		
Polygonum cuspidatum	Japanese knotweed		
Poncirus trifoliata	Hardy orange		
Potamogeton crispus	Curly pondweed		
Pueraria montana var. lobata	Kudzu		
Pyrus calleryana	Callery pear		
Salvinia molesta	Kariba-weed		
Securigera varia	Crownvetch		
Solanum viarum	Tropical soda apple		
Sphenoclea zeylanica	Chickenspike		
Tamarix ramosissima	Saltcedar		
Torilis arvensis	Spreading hedgeparsley		
Triadica sebifera	Chinese tallow		
Typha angustifolia	Narrowleaf cattail		
Ulmus pumila	Siberian elm		
Wisteria floribunda	Japanese wisteria		
Wisteria sinensis	Chinese wisteria		

* = native species included during invasive exotic plant surveys

9

Table 2. Overview of invasive exotic plants found on Pea Ridge National Military Park. Ecological impact and general management difficulty based on NatureServe I-Rank subranks, Morse et al. 2004. Subranks are given as high (H), medium (M), low (L), insignificant (I), unknown (U), a range of ranks (indicated by /), or not available (--).

Species	Common Name	Watch list	Park-wide cover (acres)	Frequency (percent)	Ecological impact	Management difficulty
Juniperus virginiana	Eastern redcedar	Park-based	671.8 – 1151.7	42.8	----	----
Lespedeza cuneata	Sericea lespedeza	Park-established	6.8 – 19.9	19.1	ML	ML
Lonicera japonica	Japanese honeysuckle	Park-established	2.9 – 13.9	18.5	M	HM
Rosa multiflora	Multiflora rose	Park-established	2.2 – 9.2	19.1	L	L
Lolium spp	Fescue	Early-detection	0.8 – 2.7	5.2	----	----
Microstegium vimineum	Nepalese browntop	Early-detection	0.3 – 2.1	8.1	M	HM
Robinia pseudoacacia	Black locust	Park-established	0.3 – 1.6	6.4	HM	M
Sorghum halepense	Johnsongrass	Park-established	0.2 – 1.1	3.5	ML	HM
Centaurea stoebe ssp. micranthos	Spotted knapweed	Early-detection	< 0.75	2.9	M	HL
Dactylis glomerata	Orchardgrass	Park-established	< 0.75	5.2	LI	ML
Verbascum thapsus	Common mullein	Park-established	< 0.25	2.3	ML	L
Ligustrum spp	Smooth brome	Early-detection	< 0.1	0.6	M	ML
Bromus inermis	Privet	Early-detection	< 0.01	1.7	----	----
Poa compressa	Canada bluegrass	Early-detection	< 0.01	0.6	ML	HL

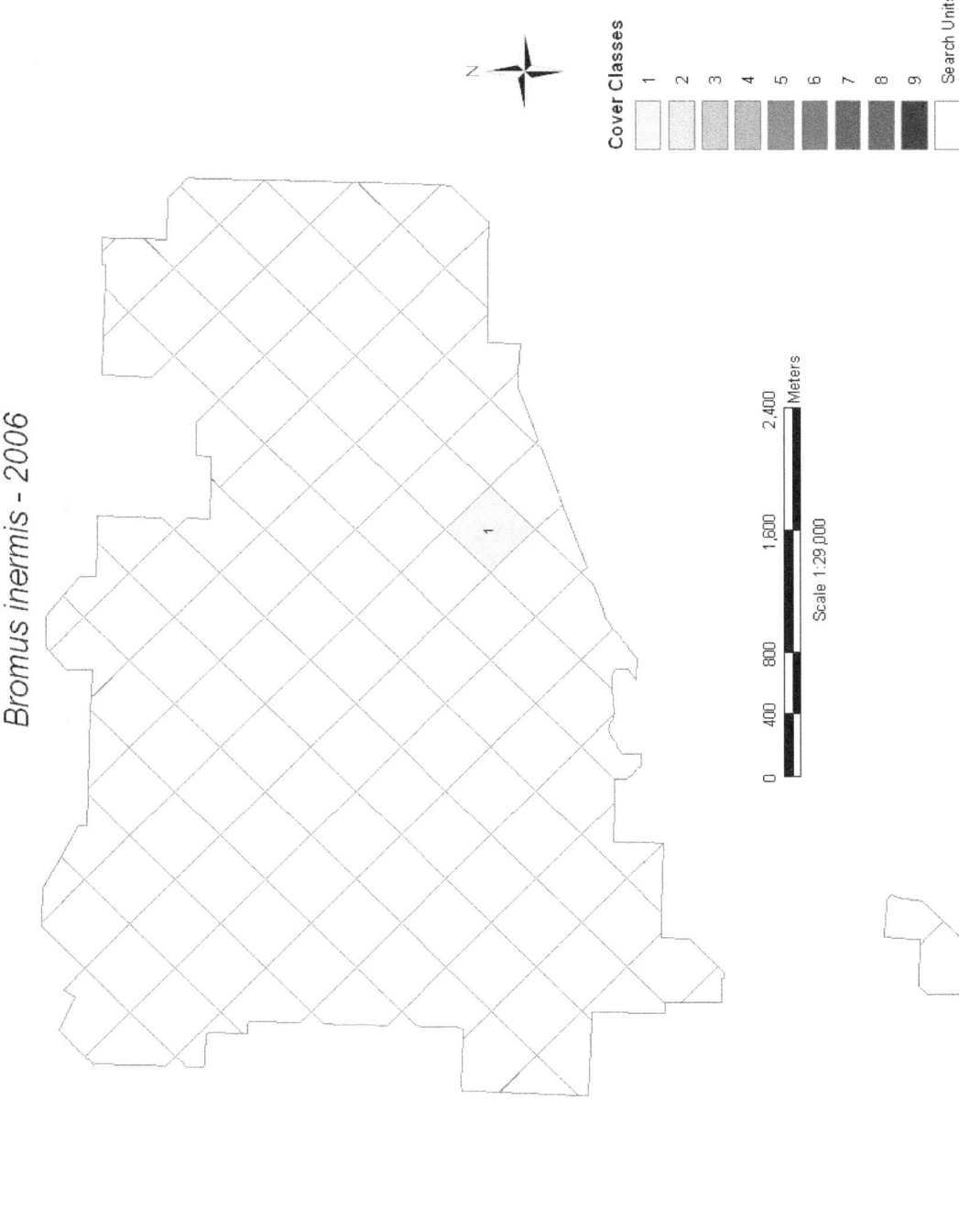

Bromus inermis - 2006

Cover Classes
1
2
3
4
5
6
7
8
9
Search Units

Scale 1:29,000

0   400   800   1,600   2,400
Meters

Figure 2. Abundance and distribution of *Bromus inermis* (smooth brome) at Pea Ridge National Military Park, 2006. Cover classes are as follows: 1=0.1-0.9 m^2, 2=1-9.9 m^2, 3=10-49.9 m^2, 4= 50-99.9 m^2, 5=100-499.9 m^2, 6= 499.9-999.9 m^2, 7=1,000-4,999.9 m^2, 8=5,000-9,999.9 m^2, and 9=10,000-14,999.9 m^2. See figure 1 for areas searched.

Centaurea stoebe ssp micranthos - 2006

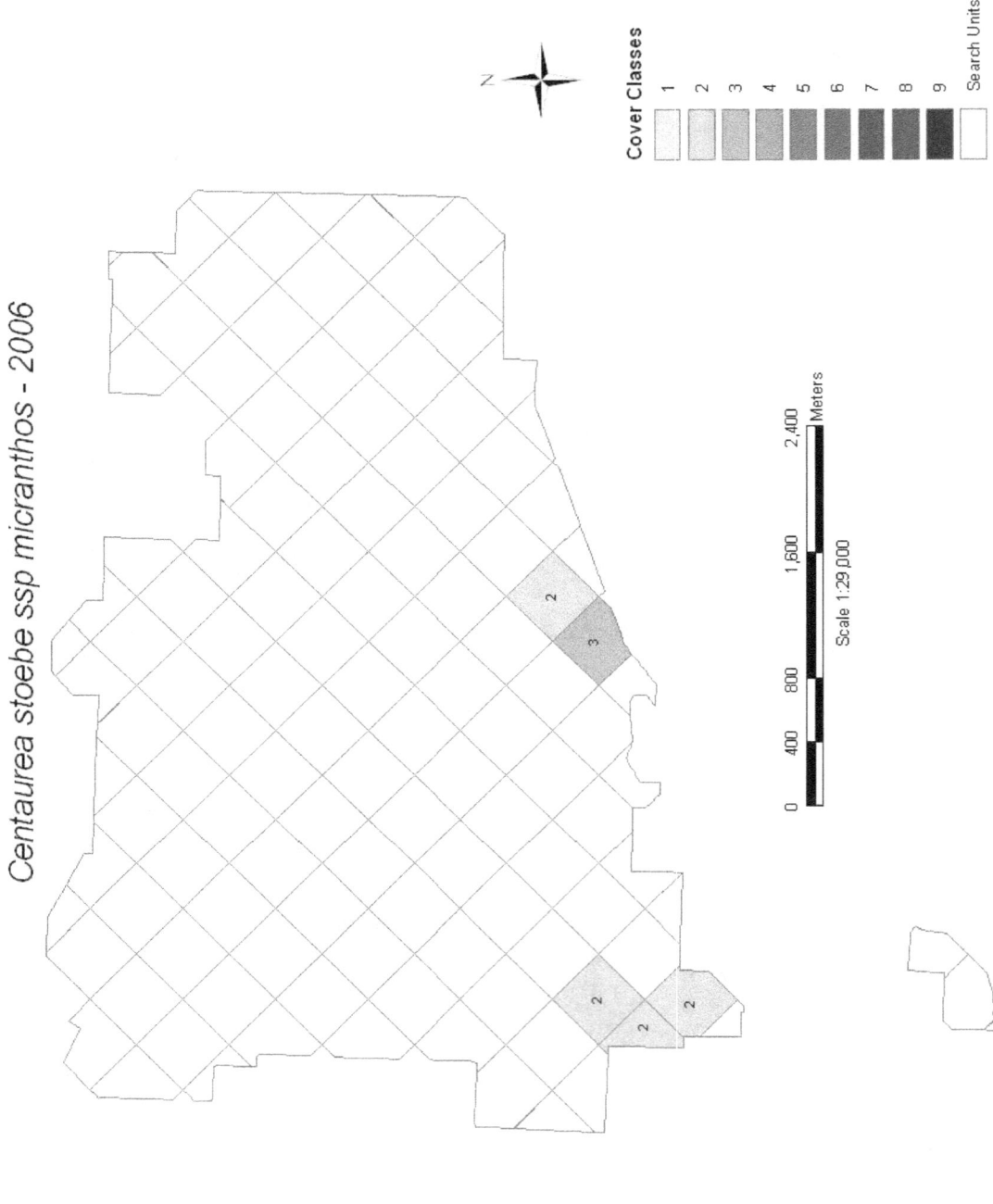

Figure 3. Abundance and distribution of *Centaurea stoebe ssp. micranthos* (spotted knapweed) at Pea Ridge National Military Park, 2006. Cover classes are as follows: 1=0.1-0.9 m^2, 2=1-9.9 m^2, 3=10-49.9 m^2, 4= 50-99.9 m^2, 5=100-499.9 m^2, 6= 499.9-999.9 m^2, 7=1,000-4,999.9 m^2, 8=5,000-9,999.9 m^2, and 9=10,000-14,999.9 m^2. See figure 1 for areas searched.

Dactylis glomerata - 2006

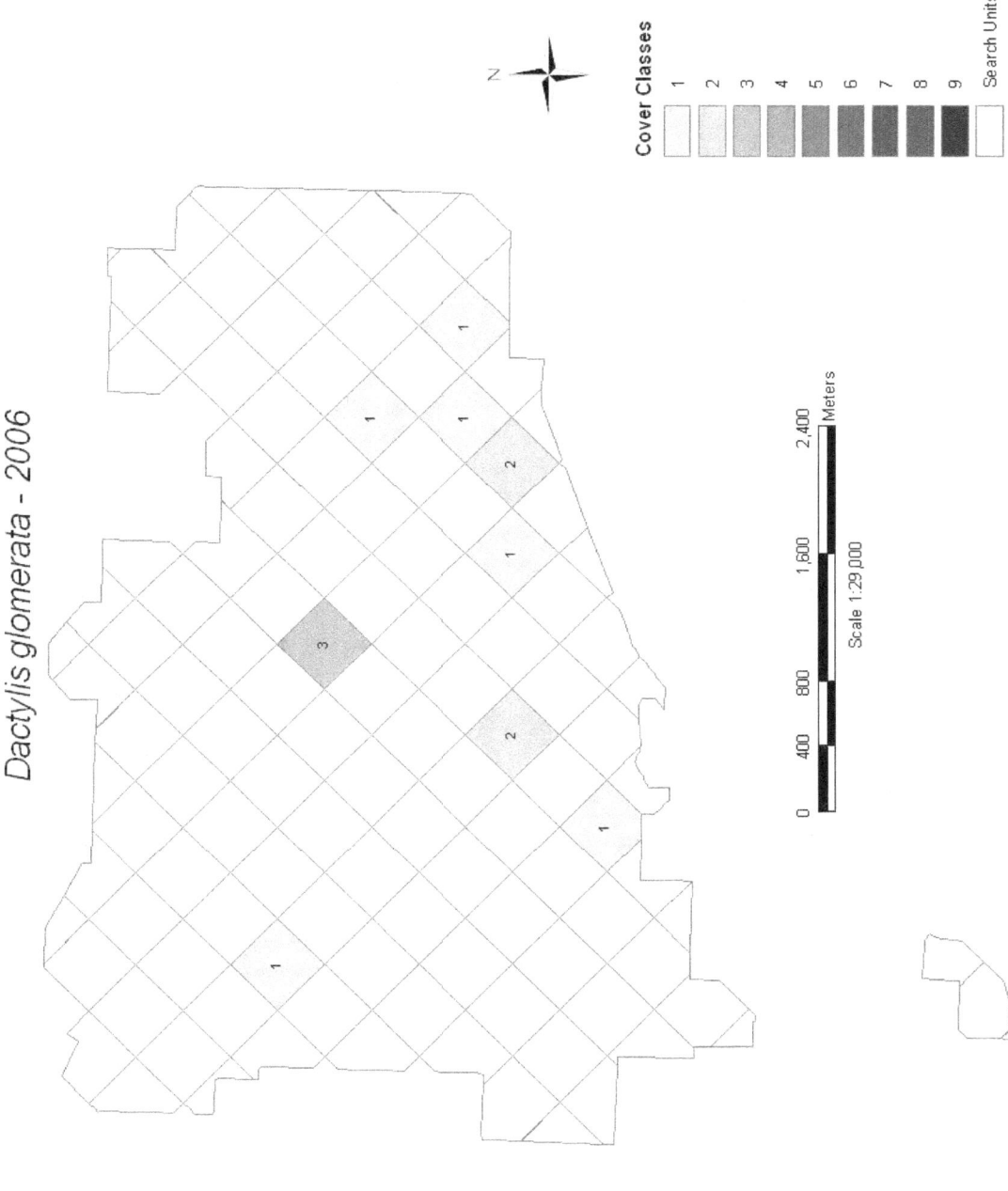

Cover Classes
1
2
3
4
5
6
7
8
9

Search Units

N

Scale 1:29,000

0   400   800   1,600   2,400
Meters

Figure 4. Abundance and distribution of *Dactylis glomerata* (orchardgrass) at Pea Ridge National Military Park, 2006. Cover classes are as follows: 1=0.1-0.9 m^2, 2=1-9.9 m^2, 3=10-49.9 m^2, 4= 50-99.9 m^2, 5=100-499.9 m^2, 6= 499.9-999.9 m^2, 7=1,000-4,999.9 m^2, 8=5,000-9,999.9 m^2, and 9=10,000-14,999.9 m^2. See figure 1 for areas searched.

Juniperus virginianus - 2006

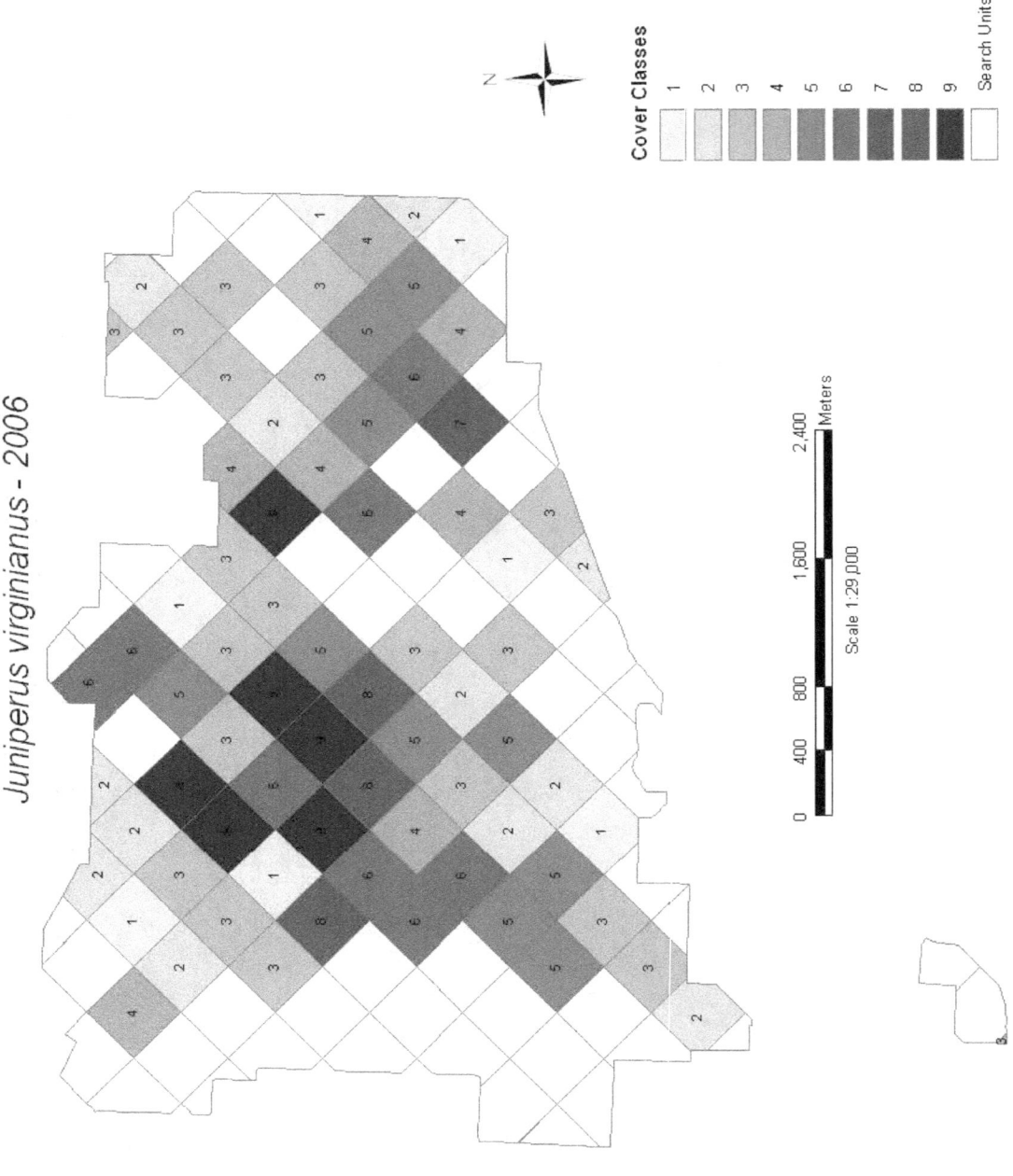

Figure 5. Abundance and distribution of *Juniperus virginiana* (eastern redcedar) at Pea Ridge National Military Park, 2006. Cover classes are as follows: 1=0.1-0.9 m², 2=1-9.9 m², 3=10-49.9 m², 4= 50-99.9 m², 5=100-499.9 m², 6= 499.9-999.9 m², 7=1,000-4,999.9 m², 8=5,000-9,999.9 m², and 9=10,000-14,999.9 m². See figure 1 for areas searched.

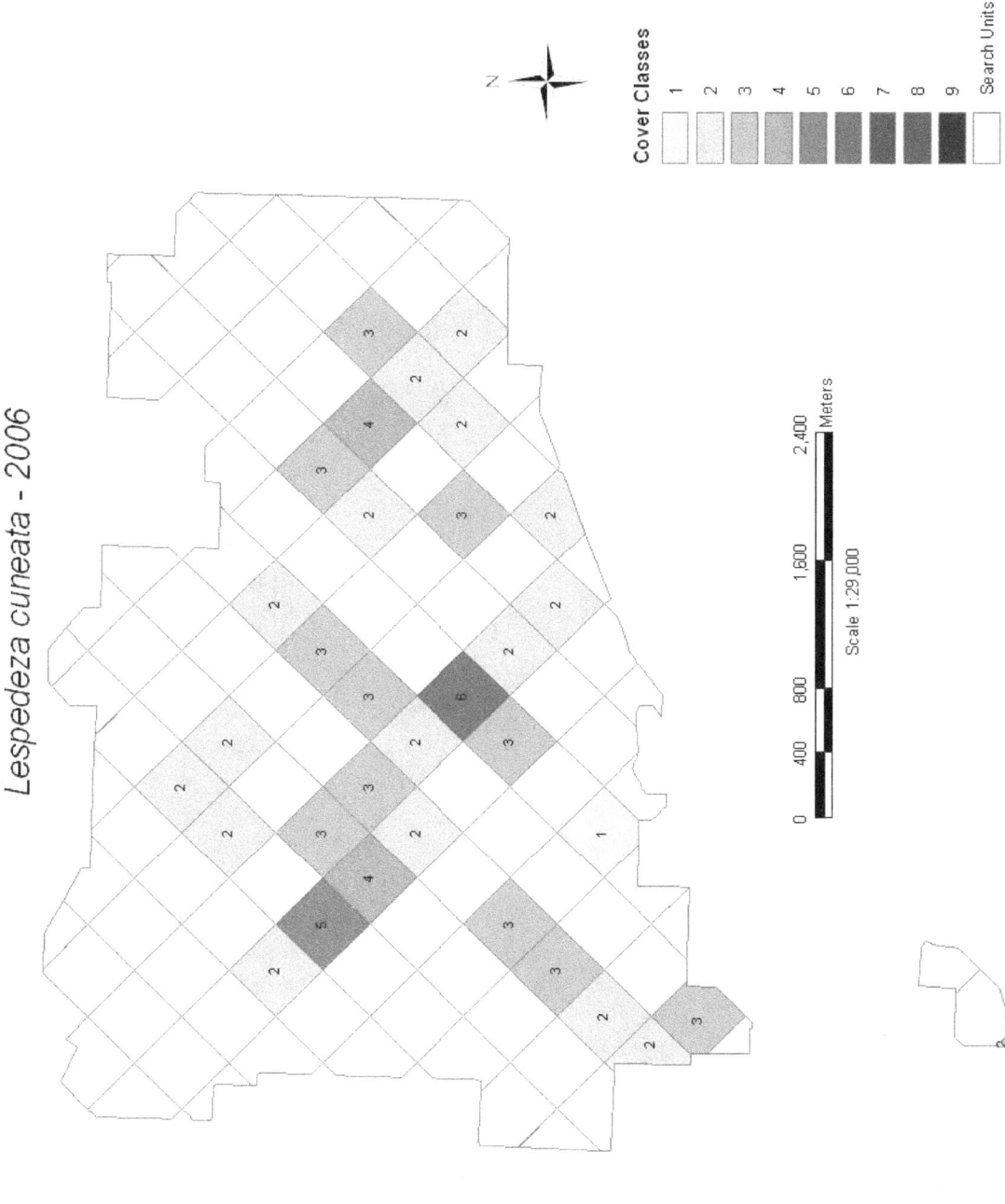

Lespedeza cuneata - 2006

Figure 6. Abundance and distribution of *Lespedeza cuneata* (sericea lespedeza) at Pea Ridge National Military Park, 2006. Cover classes are as follows: 1=0.1-0.9 m^2, 2=1-9.9 m^2, 3=10-49.9 m^2, 4= 50-99.9 m^2, 5=100-499.9 m^2, 6= 499.9-999.9 m^2, 7=1,000-4,999.9 m^2, 8=5,000-9,999.9 m^2, and 9=10,000-14,999.9 m^2. See figure 1 for areas searched.

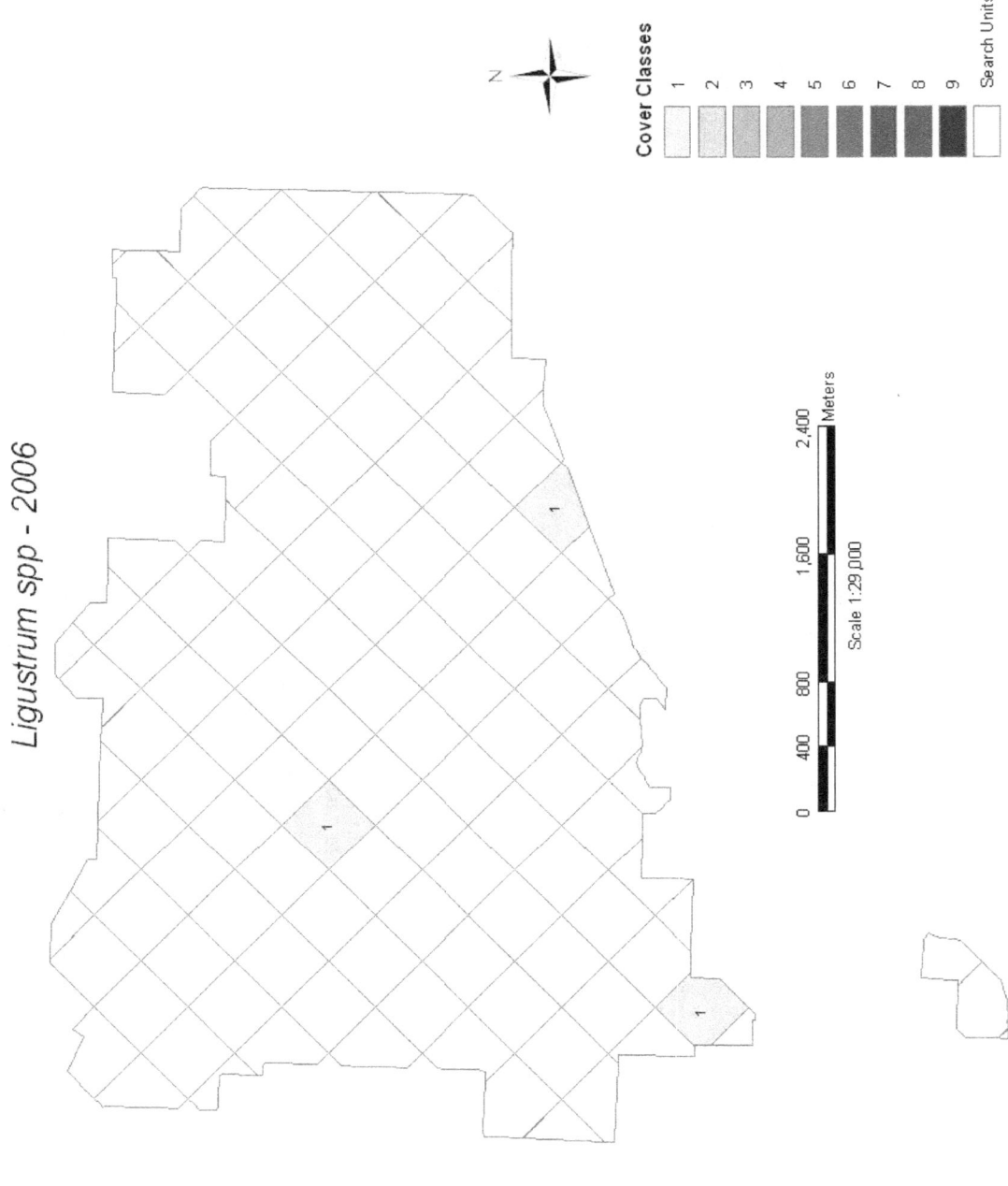

Ligustrum spp - 2006

Figure 7. Abundance and distribution of *Ligustrum spp* (privet) at Pea Ridge National Military Park, 2006. Cover classes are as follows: $1=0.1-0.9$ m^2, $2=1-9.9$ m^2, $3=10-49.9$ m^2, $4=50-99.9$ m^2, $5=100-499.9$ m^2, $6=499.9-999.9$ m^2, $7=1,000-4,999.9$ m^2, $8=5,000-9,999.9$ m^2, and $9=10,000-14,999.9$ m^2. See figure 1 for areas searched.

Lonicera japonica - 2006

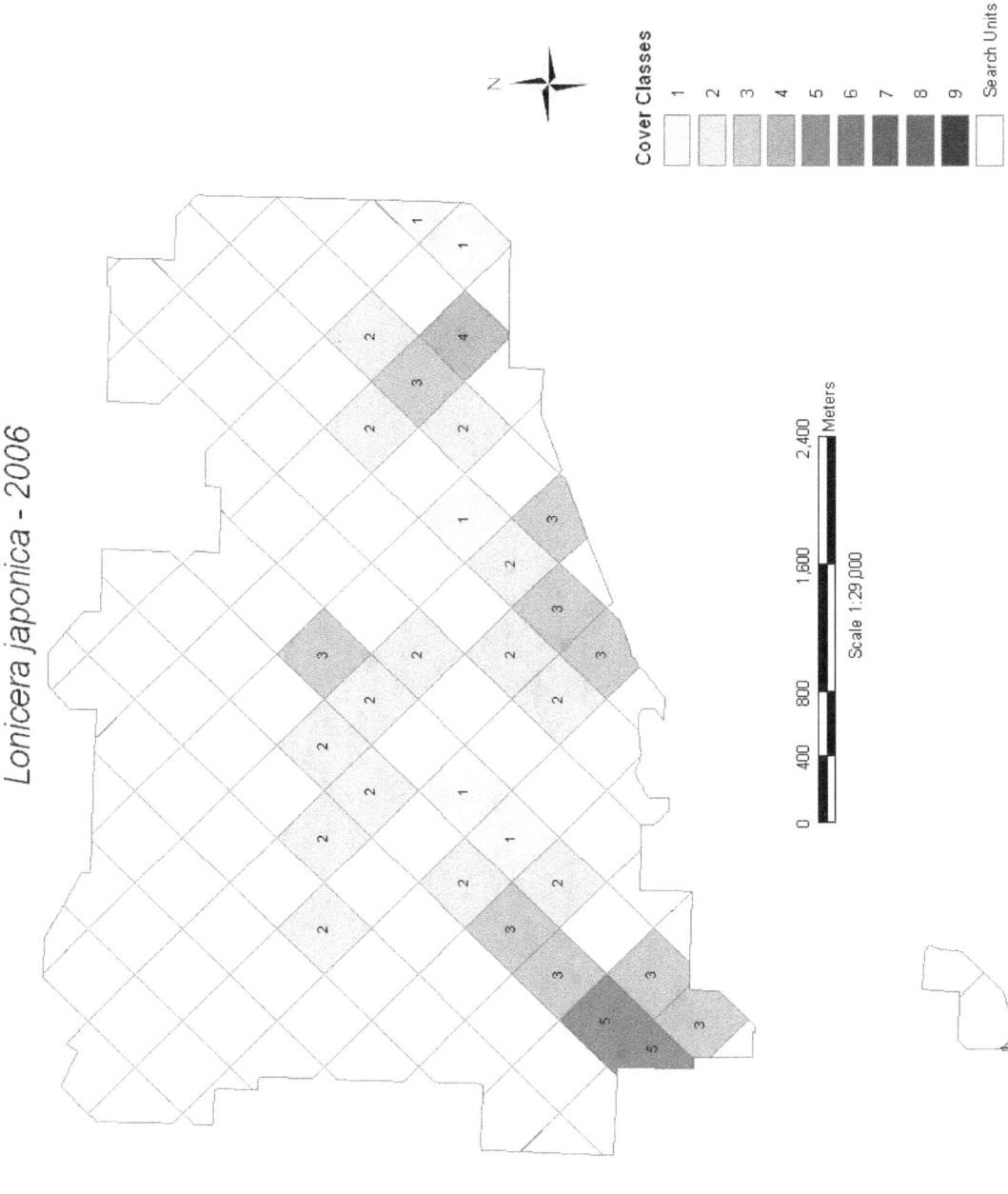

Figure 8. Abundance and distribution of *Lonicera japonica* **(Japanese honeysuckle) at Pea Ridge National Military Park, 2006. Cover classes are as follows: 1=0.1-0.9 m², 2=1-9.9 m², 3=10-49.9 m², 4= 50-99.9 m², 5=100-499.9 m², 6= 499.9-999.9 m², 7=1,000-4,999.9 m², 8=5,000-9,999.9 m², and 9=10,000-14,999.9 m². See figure 1 for areas searched.**

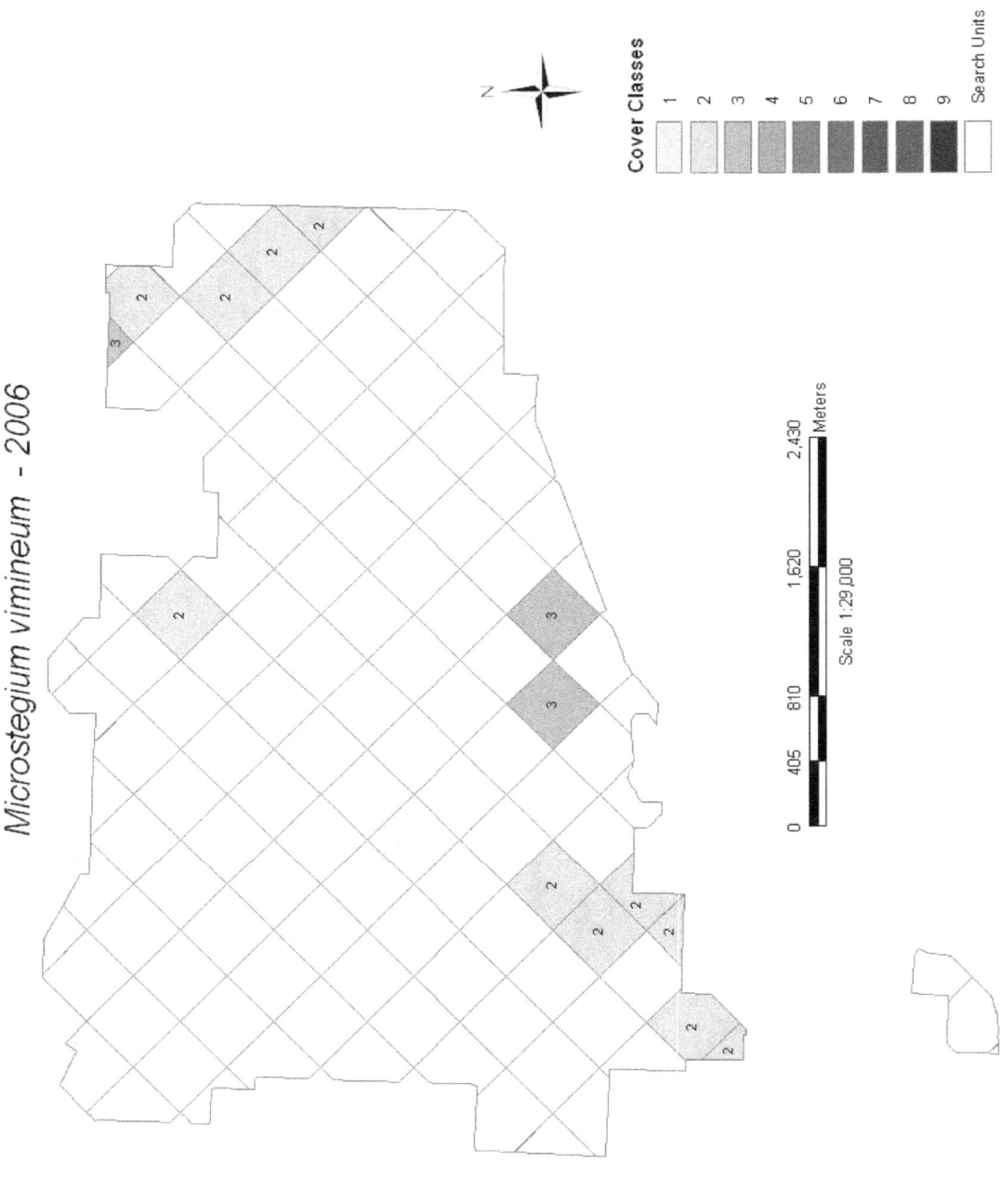

Microstegium vimineum - 2006

Figure 9. Abundance and distribution of *Microstegium vimineum* (nepalese browntop) at Pea Ridge National Military Park, 2006. Cover classes are as follows: $1=0.1\text{-}0.9$ m^2, $2=1\text{-}9.9$ m^2, $3=10\text{-}49.9$ m^2, $4=50\text{-}99.9$ m^2, $5=100\text{-}499.9$ m^2, $6=499.9\text{-}999.9$ m^2, $7=1,000\text{-}4,999.9$ m^2, $8=5,000\text{-}9,999.9$ m^2, and $9=10,000\text{-}14,999.9$ m^2. See figure 1 for areas searched.

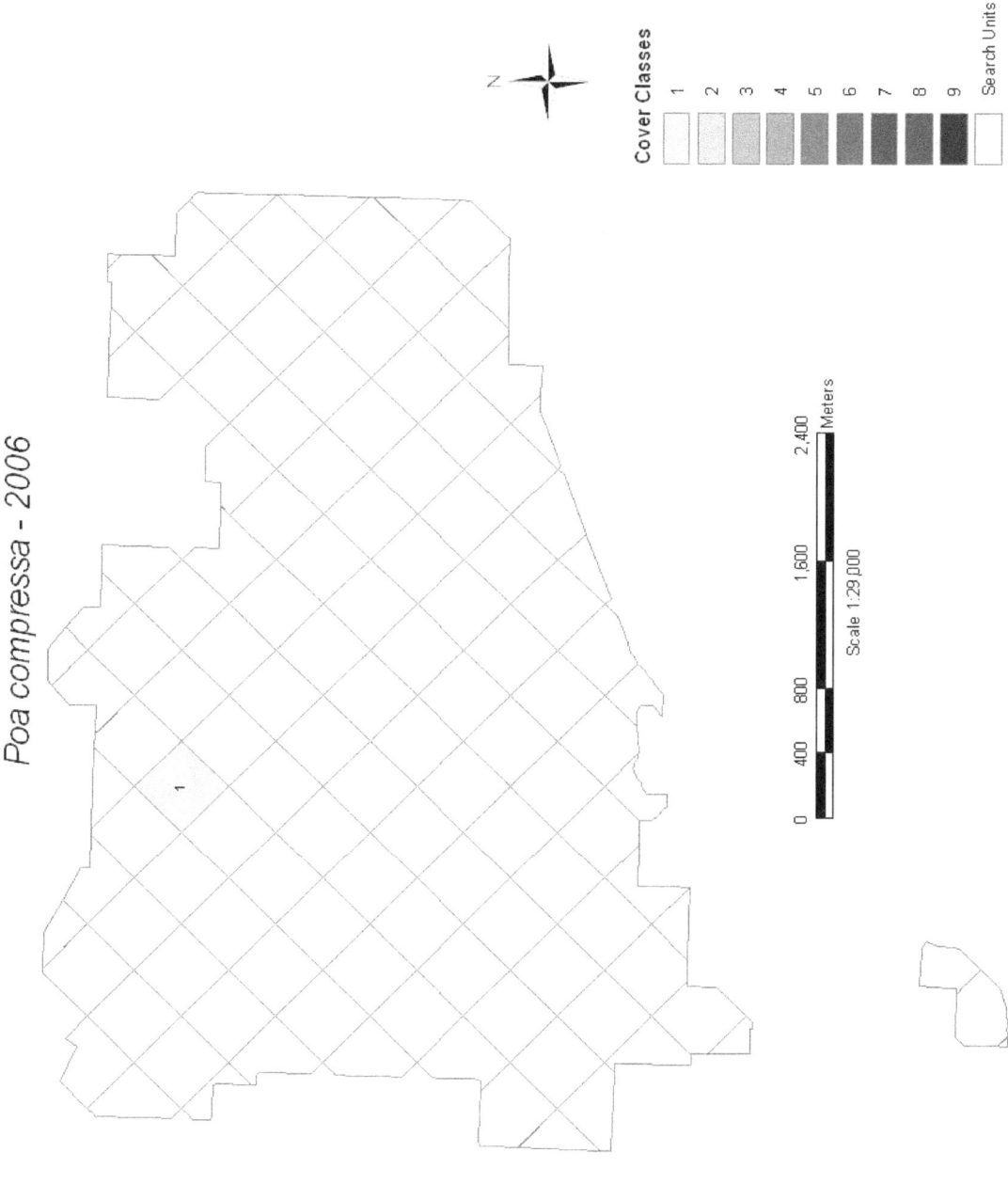

Poa compressa - 2006

Cover Classes

Search Units

Figure 10. Abundance and distribution of *Poa compressa* (canada bluegrass) at Pea Ridge National Military Park, 2006. Cover classes are as follows: 1=0.1-0.9 m², 2=1-9.9 m², 3=10-49.9 m², 4= 50-99.9 m², 5=100-499.9 m², 6= 499.9-999.9 m², 7=1,000-4,999.9 m², 8=5,000-9,999.9 m², and 9=10,000-14,999.9 m². See figure 1 for areas searched.

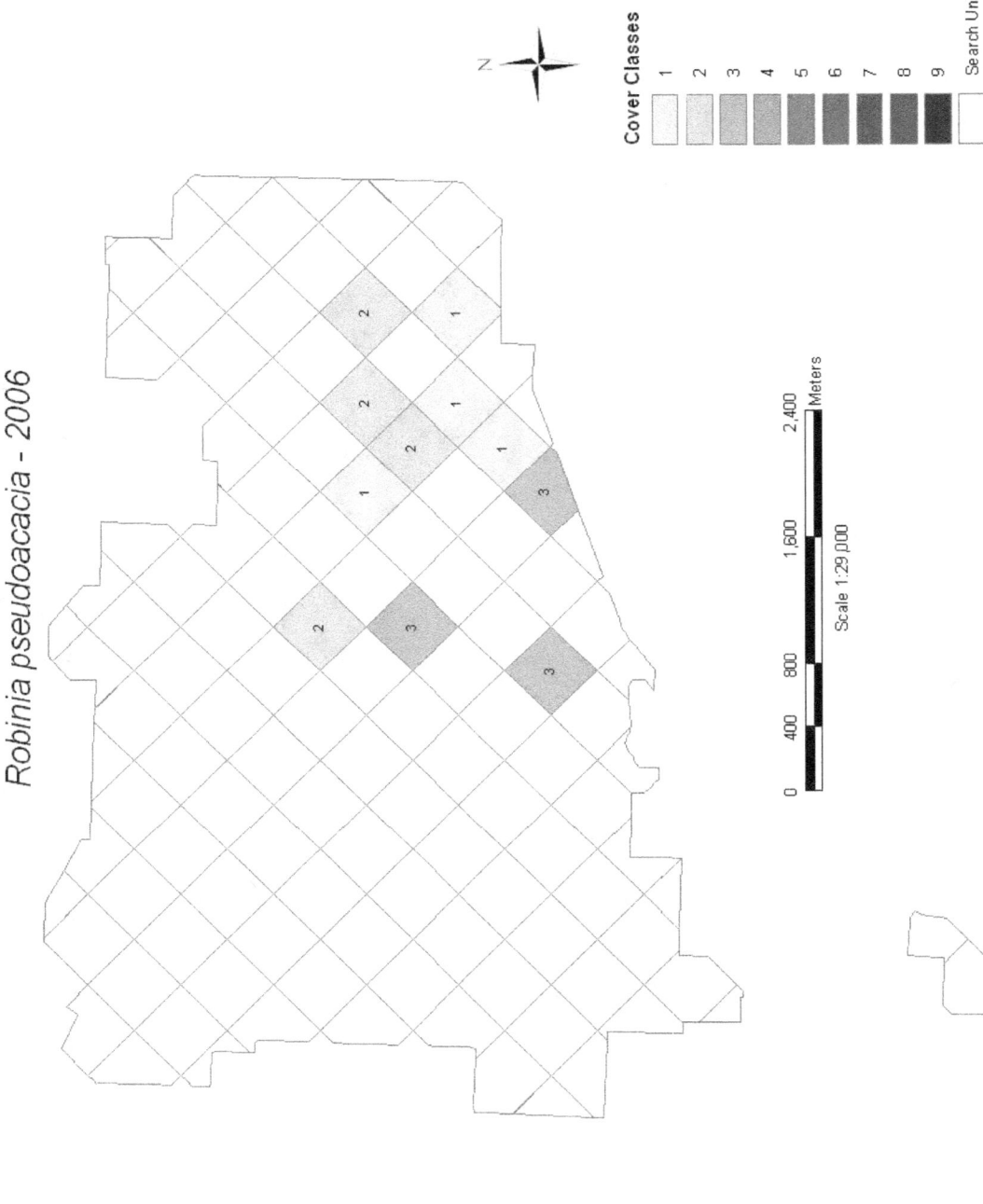

Robinia pseudoacacia - 2006

Cover Classes

1
2
3
4
5
6
7
8
9

Search Units

Scale 1:29,000

0   400   800   1,600   2,400
Meters

Figure 11. Abundance and distribution of *Robinia pseudoacacia* (black locust) at Pea Ridge National Military Park, 2006. Cover classes are as follows: 1=0.1-0.9 m², 2=1-9.9 m², 3=10-49.9 m², 4= 50-99.9 m², 5=100-499.9 m², 6= 499.9-999.9 m², 7=1,000-4,999.9 m², 8=5,000-9,999.9 m², and 9=10,000-14,999.9 m². See figure 1 for areas searched.

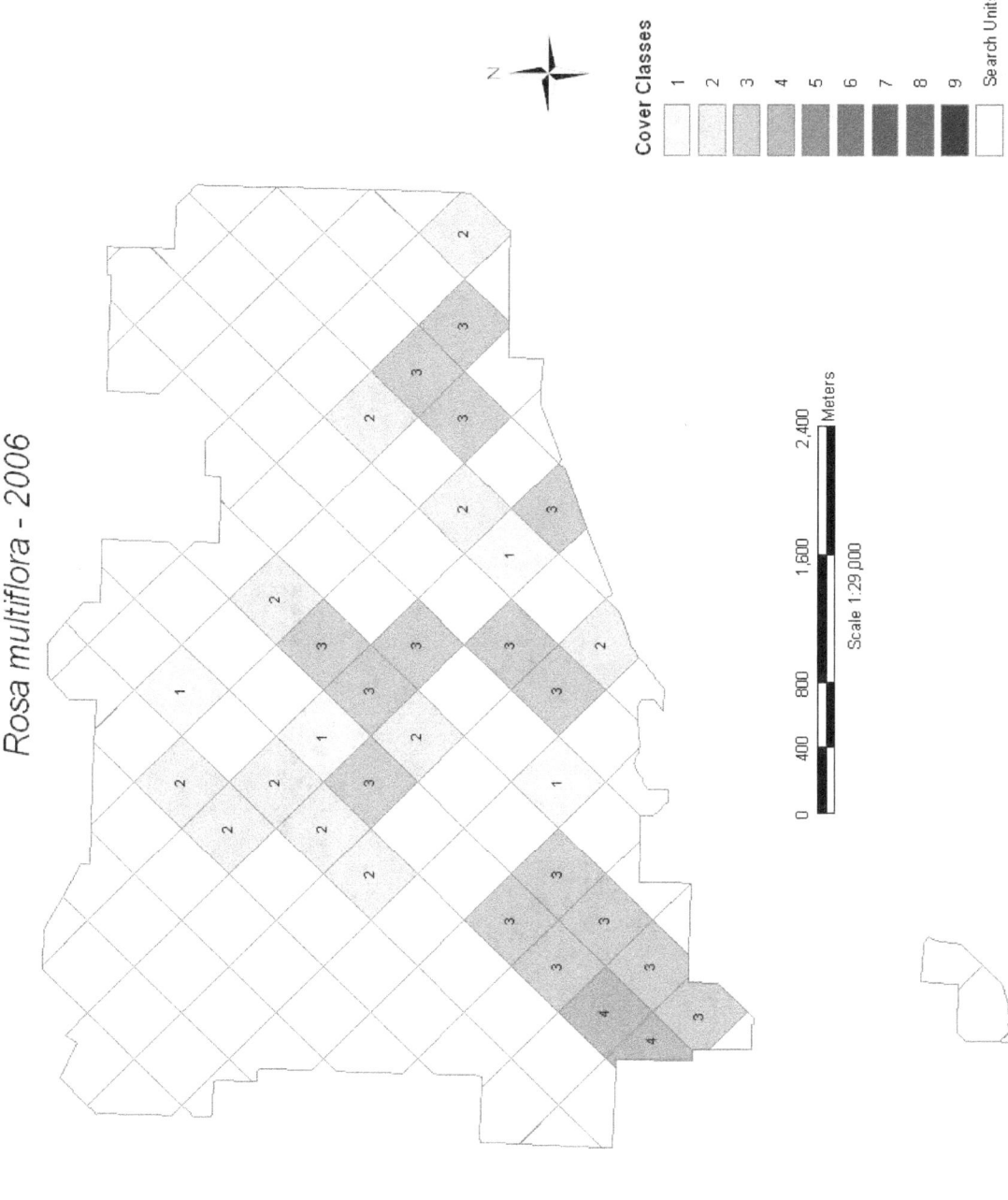

Rosa multiflora - 2006

Figure 12. Abundance and distribution of *Rosa multiflora* (multiflora rose) at Pea Ridge National Military Park, 2006. Cover classes are as follows: 1=0.1-0.9 m², 2=1-9.9 m², 3=10-49.9 m², 4= 50-99.9 m², 5=100-499.9 m², 6= 499.9-999.9 m², 7=1,000-4,999.9 m², 8=5,000-9,999.9 m², and 9=10,000-14,999.9 m². See figure 1 for areas searched.

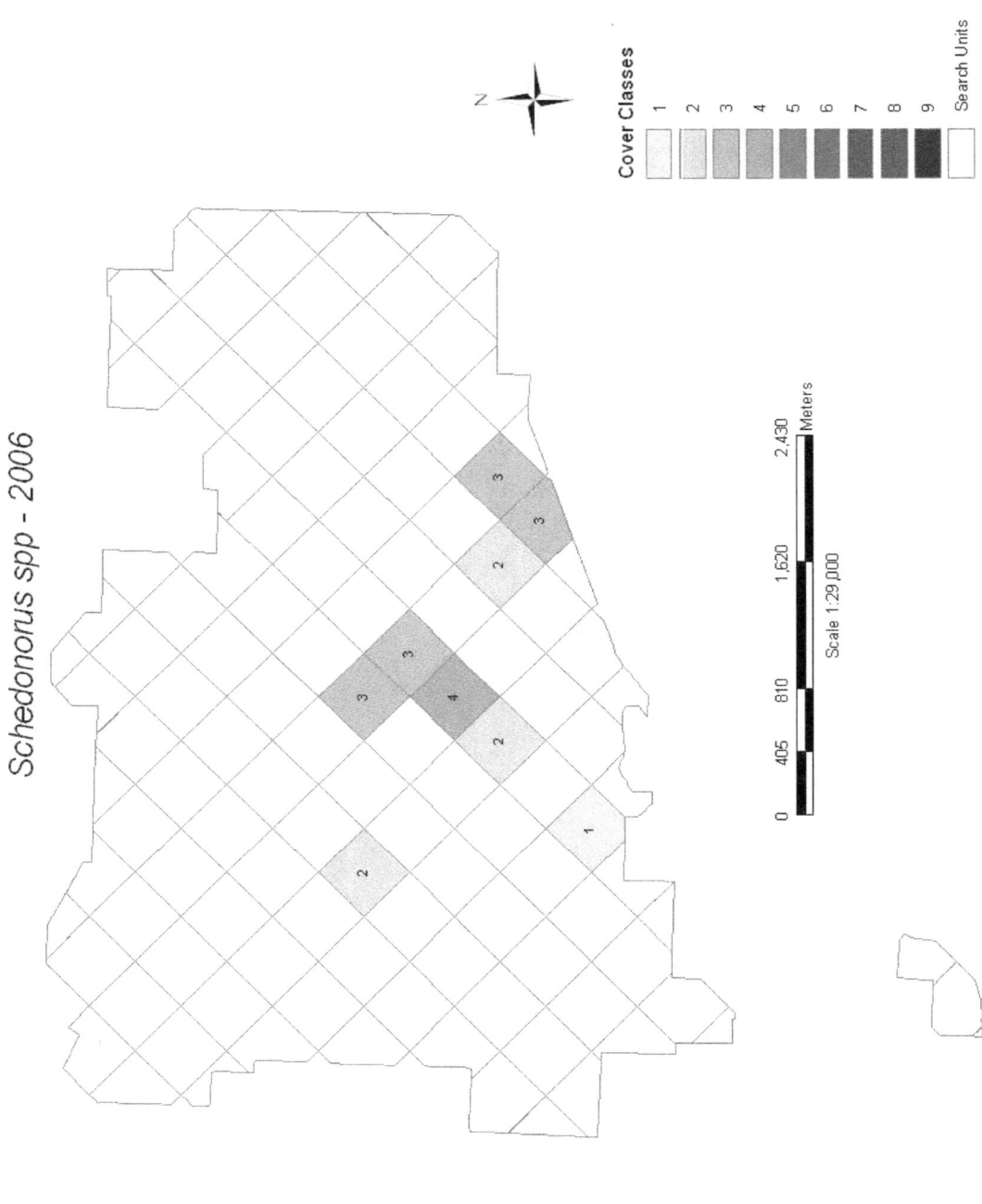

Schedonorus spp - 2006

Figure 13. Abundance and distribution of *Schedonorus* spp (fescue) at Pea Ridge National Military Park, 2006. Cover classes are as follows: $1=0.1\text{-}0.9\ m^2$, $2=1\text{-}9.9\ m^2$, $3=10\text{-}49.9\ m^2$, $4=50\text{-}99.9\ m^2$, $5=100\text{-}499.9\ m^2$, $6=499.9\text{-}999.9\ m^2$, $7=1,000\text{-}4,999.9\ m^2$, $8=5,000\text{-}9,999.9\ m^2$, and $9=10,000\text{-}14,999.9\ m^2$. See figure 1 for areas searched.

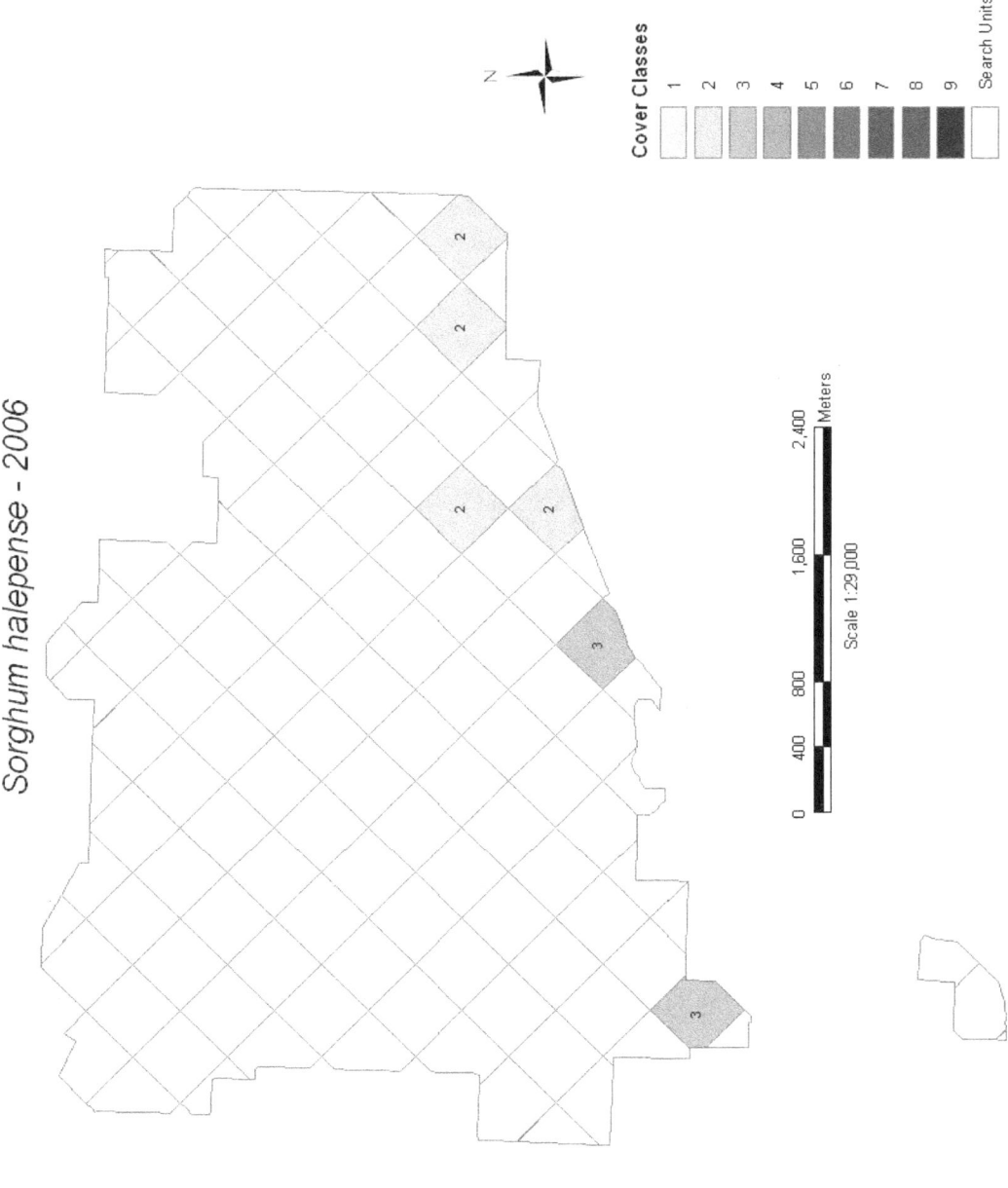

Sorghum halepense - 2006

Figure 14. Abundance and distribution of *Sorghum halepense* (Johnsongrass) at Pea Ridge National Military Park, 2006. Cover classes are as follows: 1=0.1-0.9 m², 2=1-9.9 m², 3=10-49.9 m², 4= 50-99.9 m², 5=100-499.9 m², 6= 499.9-999.9 m², 7=1,000-4,999.9 m², 8=5,000-9,999.9 m², and 9=10,000-14,999.9 m². See figure 1 for areas searched.

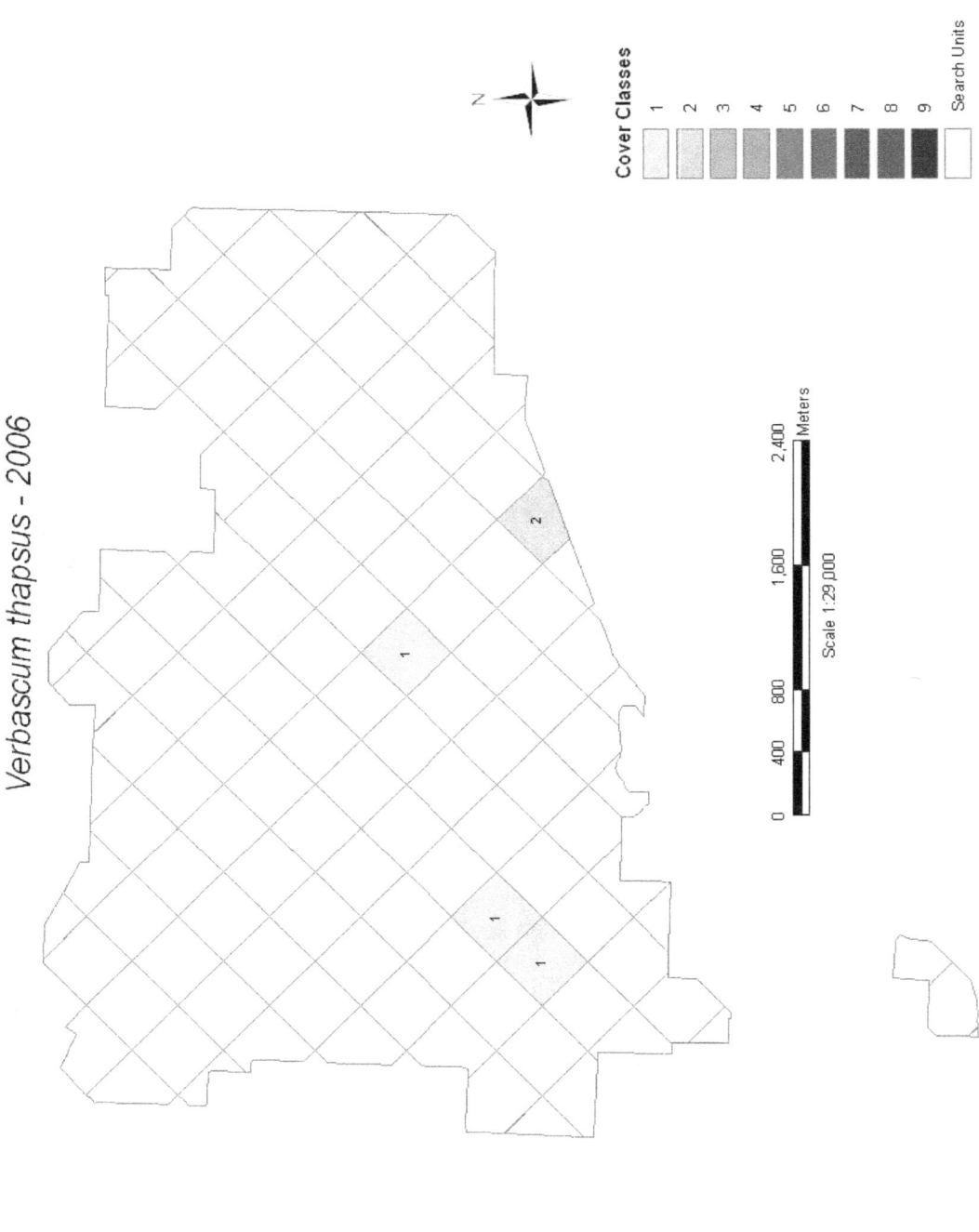

Verbascum thapsus - 2006

Figure 15. Abundance and distribution of *Verbascum thapsus* (common mullein) at Pea Ridge National Military Park, 2006. Cover classes are as follows: 1=0.1-0.9 m^2, 2=1-9.9 m^2, 3=10-49.9 m^2, 4= 50-99.9 m^2, 5=100-499.9 m^2, 6= 499.9-999.9 m^2, 7=1,000-4,999.9 m^2, 8=5,000-9,999.9 m^2, and 9=10,000-14,999.9 m^2. See figure 1 for areas searched.

The NPS has organized its parks with significant natural resources into 32 networks linked by geography and shared natural resource characteristics. HTLN is composed of 15 National Park Service (NPS) units in eight Midwestern states. These parks contain a wide variety of natural and cultural resources including sites focused on commemorating civil war battlefields, Native American heritage, westward expansion, and our U.S. Presidents. The Network is charged with creating inventories of its species and natural features as well as monitoring trends and issues in order to make sound management decisions. Critical inventories help park managers understand the natural resources in their care while monitoring programs help them understand meaningful change in natural systems and to respond accordingly. The Heartland Network helps to link natural and cultural resources by protecting the habitat of our history.

The I&M program bridges the gap between science and management with a third of its efforts aimed at making information accessible. Each network of parks, such as Heartland, has its own multi-disciplinary team of scientists, support personnel, and seasonal field technicians whose system of online databases and reports make information and research results available to all. Greater efficiency is achieved through shared staff and funding as these core groups of professionals augment work done by individual park staff. Through this type of integration and partnership, network parks are able to accomplish more than a single park could on its own.

The mission of the Heartland Network is to collaboratively develop and conduct scientifically credible inventories and long-term monitoring of park "vital signs" and to distribute this information for use by park staff, partners, and the public, thus enhancing understanding which leads to sound decision making in the preservation of natural resources and cultural history held in trust by the National Park Service.

www.nature.nps.gov/im/units/htln/

Heartland
Network
Natural Resource Monitoring

The U.S. Department of the Interior (DOI) is the nation's principal conservation agency, charged with the mission "*to protect and provide access to our Nation's natural and cultural heritage and honor our trust responsibilities to Indian tribes and our commitments to island communities.*" More specifically, Interior protects America's treasures for future generations, provides access to our nation's natural and cultural heritage, offers recreation opportunities, honors its trust responsibilities to American Indians and Alaska Natives and its responsibilities to island communities, conducts scientific research, provides wise stewardship of energy and mineral resources, fosters sound use of land and water resources, and conserves and protects fish and wildlife. The work that we do affects the lives of millions of people; from the family taking a vacation in one of our national parks to the children studying in one of our Indian schools.

NPS D-49, March 2007

www.ingramcontent.com/pod-product-compliance
Lightning Source LLC
Chambersburg PA
CBHW080939290526
45795CB00007BA/2821